FEARLESS FOUNDATIONS

Your Blueprint to Real Estate Development

Ryan Duffy, Ryan Meuer, Jordan Holmes, Mike Sebastian, Vinci Sevilla Jr., Andrew Boer, and Bill Beck

CASH STREET
ADVISORS PRESS
GET PUBLISHED ON MONEY STREET

Cash Street Advisors Press

First published in 2025 by Cash Street Advisors Press LLC

ISBN # Paper: 979-8-9887875-8-7
ISBN # EBook: 979-8-9887875-7-0

Library of Congress Control Number: 2025935295

Printed in the United States of America

Editing by James Douglas
Book Cover and Formatting Design by Kristina Conatser | www.capturedbykcdesigns.com

 Disclaimer:

<u>Dedication</u>

To all the real estate investors bold enough to dream big, take risks, and build their own *Fearless Foundations*.

This book is for the visionaries, the action-takers, and the re-silient souls who refuse to let fear hold them back. May your courage inspire others, your efforts pave the way for lasting impact, and your success serve as a testament to what's possible when you dare to believe in yourself.

Keep building, keep growing, and keep living fearlessly.
This is your legacy.

CONTENTS

INTRODUCTION

Welcome to the exciting world of real estate development where fortunes are made by those bold enough to see beyond the surface and seize opportunities others overlook. In *Fearless Foundations*, we embark on a journey that transcends traditional notions of real estate investment. This book is not just about buying and selling properties; it's about embracing risk, uncovering hidden value, and ultimately achieving prosperity in the dynamic landscape of real estate development.

Each chapter of this book is meticulously crafted to provide you with insights, strategies, and real-world examples that will empower you to navigate the complexities of real estate investing with confidence and clarity. Whether you're a risk-taker seeking high returns or a conservative investor looking to expand your horizons, there's something here for you.

So join us as we delve into navigating the thrilling world of risk, uncover hidden gems, and master the art of balancing risk with reward. Together, let's embark on a journey towards real estate riches.

Calculated Growth: The Power of Data in Real Estate

by Ryan Meuer

"What would you do if this were your company, losing money every month?"

At just 22 years old, I found myself in a middle management position at a Fortune 500 company sitting in my boss's office. He was frustrated after I presented irrefutable evidence that the task he had assigned me was impossible given our limited payroll allocation. With not enough people to complete the work, I had compiled a monstrous spreadsheet—meticulously organized and color-coded—after three months of gathering data from seven different departments. It was proof of what I already instinctively knew: we were falling behind by 50 hours of work every single day.

My boss seemed indifferent. It wasn't that he couldn't understand my spreadsheet; it was that he didn't want to confront the uncomfortable truth. He had tasked me with maintaining the day-to-day operations of a large distribution center with 75 employees when we truly needed a minimum of 81.

"Just get it done," he would say.

He tossed the spreadsheet back at me, scoffing, "Well, what would you do if this were your company, losing money every month?"

Although it was a rhetorical question, I replied, "If it were my company, it wouldn't be losing money."

Shortly thereafter, I secured the additional staff I needed and received a promotion. I had proven my ability to get the job done, driven by data.

Little did I know, I was only months away from becoming a business owner myself. We purchased two NAPA Auto Parts stores in Missouri. Our ability to afford the acquisition stemmed from the smart real estate investment we had made with our primary home, selling just before the 2008 market crash.

While this may sound promising, we bought our multi-location business just as the economy and job market were collapsing. We struggled immensely, losing over $200,000 in our first two years. You know the saying, "Most businesses fail in the first five years"? It felt like we were on track to join that statistic.

We worked tirelessly, often falling into the trap of working in the business instead of on it—putting in 12-16 hour days that were mostly unproductive, filled with low-value tasks like checking out customers or shuttling parts between our stores. We found ourselves in a situation akin to that day in my boss's office: an impossible task within sufficient resources, and a relentless push to just get it done. Ironically, I had become a hypocrite; we were losing money, and fast.

I wish I could say that I had a moment of clarity and realized we needed to focus on the business itself rather than getting bogged down in the day-to-day tasks. That realization came years later, influenced by reading *Deep Work* by Cal Newport and *The 4-Hour Workweek* by Tim Ferriss. I was squandering precious time being "busy" instead of engaging in the meaningful work that would grow our business. This led to a fresh start. I began to truly analyze our numbers to drive a successful venture. Through some strategic relocations and additional acquisitions, our business turned profitable. After a decade of gradual growth, we soared in the last five years, eventually selling our stores at the beginning of 2023 following several consecutive banner years.

What I haven't mentioned is that during those last five years, my wife and I had already decided to transition to a different industry. We had exhausted our time in the auto parts business and yearned for something new. We remembered our previous work in a large property management company, *Trammell Crow Residential Services*, and how real estate had initially allowed us to enter business ownership in the first place.

Though it wasn't instantaneous, we gradually honed in on real estate as our new direction. Starting in 2016, I immersed myself in books and podcasts focused on real estate, business, and marketing, meticulously collecting data and insights to inform our journey. After successfully acquiring our first 2 properties, we had the proof of concept we needed, reinforcing the importance of knowing our numbers as we transitioned into full-time real estate investing. Coincidentally—if you believe in such things—our agent also mentioned an off-market abandoned campground for sale, which marked the exciting beginning of our journey into developing our first RV and glamping resort.

What Does It Take to Tackle a Ground-Up Development Project or New Business Venture?

Here Are My Top Five Tips after nearly 2 decades of experience, and several acquisitions and start ups.

1. **Know Your Numbers**: Understanding your numbers is paramount; tips 2-5 will all build upon this foundation.

2. **Know Your Customer Base**: Identify your low-hanging fruit and where the majority of your income will come from.

3. **Take the Time to Do Your Research**: Time is money, but poorly spent time is a wasted investment.

4. **Start Building Relationships Now**: You'll need allies and support.

5. **Begin with the End in Min**: Define your goals; without them, you're aimlessly wandering.

6. **Bonus Tip**: If you can't pay someone to do it, it's probably not a good deal.

Tip#1: Know Your Numbers

As mentioned, knowing your numbers is the most crucial aspect of any business endeavor. On one side of this coin lies the "trust your gut" crowd, which I sometimes strive to listen to; however, it should never apply to the foundational aspects of starting or expanding a business. So, how do you familiarize yourself with your numbers? There are no shortcuts to knowledge and wisdom—none of us are King Solomon. It requires time and effort or, at times, the investment in a feasibility study conducted by someone else. When planning our first ground-up build, I dedicated hundreds of hours to scrutinizing details. With this information, I could create a robust business plan and underwriting spreadsheets.

Here's a sample list of essential details to know about your business, drawn from the business plan I developed for The Embers.

- Proforma
- 5-Year Annual Cash Flow and Expenses
- Sources of Income
- Assumptions
- Glamping Tent Projected Monthly Income
- Expense Breakdown
- Monthly Cash Flow
- Links to Full Spreadsheets
- Registered Name and Corporate Structure
- Sources of Funds
- Uses of Funds
- Capital Contributions
- Total Project Funds
- Unit CapEx Breakdown
- Non-Unit CapEx Breakdown
- Break-even Analysis
- Exit Strategy
- Marketing Plan
- Industry Analysis
- Economic Outlook
- Potential Expansion

This plan significantly contributed to securing the bank funding we needed. Our bank's VP of RV Park and Campsite Financing discusses funding our project in this podcast episode of *Glampitect*. *https://youtu.be/uMFXem4ORKo?si=VeHrZdhXGO1o2FNQ*

Tip#2: Know Your Customer Base

How often do we see entrepreneurs struggle with their real estate projects or businesses? A major reason most businesses fail within their first two years is that they neglect to truly understand their customer base. **Please**, do not start building simply because you own the land. You must know who will be buying your product and assess the market potential.

Consider the following questions: How many people are visiting your market? What demand exists for what you plan to offer? These are essential queries that require honest answers.

Currently, my team and I focus on acquiring value-add RV parks, mobile home parks, and resorts. In my underwriting, I frequently encounter properties that have fallen into disrepair due to a lack of a defined customer base. Owners often build in isolated areas and spend years exhausting themselves trying to make their ventures work. This isn't a "Field of Dreams" scenario; it is not about building it and hoping they will come.

If you're uncertain about your target demographic, conduct market research. More often than not, you won't be the first to have your idea, so visit the competition.

Observe who frequents their establishments: If they are slow, what factors contribute to that? If they are busy, what attracts customers? Analyze the market landscape and evaluate future trends. Is your concept a passing fad, or does it hold long-term potential for residual income?

Tip #3: Take the Time to Do Your Research

Invest the time necessary to understand every facet of your business and your build. Rushing can be detrimental. While there will be moments that require quick decision-making—success stories often emerge from seizing opportunities—these instances should not occur during the planning phase. You should only act quickly if you have the experience to trust your instincts.

Refer to the list from Tip #1. Be prepared to answer questions from banks or partners about your Average Daily Rate (ADR) and the reasoning behind it.

1. What is your exit strategy?

2. How will you source contractors?

3. Have you accounted for additional payroll taxes?

4. What will you do if your project requires unexpected expenses, like $350 per hour for rock breaking?

5. Did you factor in losses from credit card processing fees?

6. How are your carry costs being funded during start up?

Questions like these are critical and require thorough consideration. I always encourage my partners to challenge my plans—it's better to identify potential issues now rather than later. Take the time to master the details or consult someone who can.

Additionally, you should have the following details in your business plan:

- Summary of Loan Request
- Ownership Team
- Project Vision
- Sample Layout
- Pricing and Product Placement
- Current Condition and Use of the Property
- Location and Photos
- Market Research
- Competition and Feasibility
- Management Team

Tip#4: Start Building Relationships Now

How will you find and finance your deals? What builders and contractors do you know? My advice: start cultivating genuine relationships today. Every successful deal and partnership I've established has stemmed from networking and building authentic connections. This doesn't mean every acquaintance will become a close friend, but it involves fostering genuine conversations based on shared interests.

For many, this is easier said than done. Personally, I often find it challenging, but my wife excels in this area. When we need to bring partners into a deal, she paves the way, and then I dive into the numbers. However, she can't always be present, so I continually work to improve my networking skills by reading books like *How to Win Friends and Influence People* by Dale Carnegie, *Never Eat Alone* by Keith Ferrazzi, and *The 2-Hour Cocktail Party* by Nick Gray. I put these concepts into practice, even if it feels uncomfortable.

Many people say, "I'm an introvert." I understand, because I am too. But we must embrace discomfort and engage in difficult conversations anyway. I firmly believe that success often correlates with a willingness to tackle the tough. If you can't navigate social settings, how will you manage giving difficult news to clients or partners?

As an example of what building relationships can do for you, I have included a current 5 year snapshot of one of my most recent deals*(refer to page 12)*. It was an off-market property spanning over 30 acres. It features a 3-acre lake at the center, 2 traditional houses, 12 mobile homes, 40 RV pads, and 16 enclosed boat storage units. We acquired it for $650,000. Even in distress it appraised as-is for $835,000 and in the first year it's projected to yield a 38% Cash on Cash return. Once renovations and stabilization are complete, I anticipate its value will exceed $2 million. Both the pocket listing and the capital partner originated from relationships cultivated months and years earlier.

Start building those relationships now!

Annual Cash Flow

Year Ending	Year 0	Year 1 3/31/25	Year 2 3/31/26	Year 3 3/31/27	Year 4 3/31/28	Year 5 3/31/29
Rental Revenue						
Gross Rent		262,320	278,059	283,725	295,074	306,877
Concessions		-	-	-	-	-
Total Rental Revenue		262,320	278,059	283,725	295,074	306,877
Other Income						
Laundry		1,456	1,689	1,723	1,757	1,793
N/A		-	-	-	-	-
N/A		-	-	-	-	-
N/A		-	-	-	-	-
N/A		-	-	-	-	-
Total Other Income		1,456	1,689	1,723	1,757	1,793
Effective Gross Revenue						
Gross Revenue		263,776	279,748	285,448	296,832	308,670
General Vacancy		(13,189)	(13,987)	(14,272)	(14,842)	(15,433)
Credit Loss		(8,573)	(9,092)	(9,277)	(9,647)	(10,032)
Total Effective Gross Revenue		242,015	256,669	261,899	272,343	283,205
Expenses						
Controllable						
Repairs and Maintenance		13,200	13,464	13,733	14,008	14,288
Contract Services		16,800	17,136	17,479	17,828	18,185
Misc Expenses		3,000	3,000	3,060	3,121	3,184
Administrative		0	0	0	0	0
Advertising and Marketing		0	0	0	0	0
Payroll		4,800	4,800	4,800	4,800	4,800
Utilities		10,800	10,800	11,016	11,236	11,461
Fixed						
Property Taxes		3,000	3,000	3,030	3,060	3,091
Insurance		12,000	12,240	12,485	12,734	12,989
Property Management		12,101	12,833	13,095	13,617	14,160
Capital Reserves		12,000	12,000	12,000	12,000	12,000
Total Expenses		87,701	89,274	90,698	92,406	94,158
NOI		154,314	167,395	171,201	179,937	189,046
Capital Expenditures						
Major Cap Ex Projects (units)		-	-	-	-	-
Major Cap Ex Projects (non-unit)		5	-	-	-	-
Total Capital Expenditures		5	-	-	-	-
CFO		154,308	167,395	171,201	179,937	189,046
Debt Service		(52,548)	(55,214)	(55,214)	(55,214)	(55,214)
CFAF		101,765	112,181	115,987	124,723	133,832
Loan						
Loan Proceeds	540,000	-	-	-	-	-
Loan Repayment		-	-	-	-	488,435
Disposition						
Sale Price		-	-	-	-	2,206,042
Sale Costs		-	-	-	-	176,483
Net Proceeds (unlevered)		-	-	-	-	2,029,559
Unlevered Cash Flow	(675,004)	154,308	167,395	171,201	179,937	2,218,605
IRR	47%					
EM	4.28x					
Levered Cash Flow	(160,001)	101,765	112,181	115,987	124,723	1,674,956
IRR	128%					
EM	13.31x					
Free and Clear	17.44%	15.08%	16.62%	17.18%	18.48%	19.83%
Cash on Cash	73.56%	63.60%	70.11%	72.49%	77.95%	83.64%
Debt Yield	28.58%	28.58%	31.00%	31.70%	33.32%	35.01%
DSCR (first column is avg)	3.15x	2.94x	3.03x	3.10x	3.26x	3.42x

Tip #5: Begin with the End in Mind

It may sound cliché, but beginning with the end in mind is essential. Identify what you want to accomplish and work toward those goals daily, integrating them into your projects and under-writing. Clearly define those goals to answer the question: *why are you pursuing this venture?* For me it's time freedom and financial freedom. To get to that freedom, I need to focus on engaging in the aspects of business I enjoy most and that are the most beneficial to growth—planning, development, and launching new projects. In order to do that, I need to scale all my operations to support the additional staff to run the day-to-day routines.

While some people thrive on owning a property and managing the day-to-day operations themselves, being tied to those daily tasks limits your ability to scale. To step away from routine responsi-bilities, I focus on pursuing properties and businesses that generate sufficient revenue to support a standalone staff, all while ensuring a worthwhile return for both myself and our investors.

Bonus Tip: If you can't pay someone to do it, it's probably not a good deal.

Do you work for free? I've seen countless people struggle with budgets, only to conclude, "I'll just do that myself." Saving money is commendable, but it's crucial to distinguish between saving costs and relying on yourself out of necessity. This principle applies across every niche. In short-term rentals, many convince themselves to self-manage in order to show a decent return, but if they plugged in the true cost of property management, their property would be losing money. In construction or house flipping, some people take on general contracting or trade work themselves to have the same effect. Never undertake the burden of day-to-day work as a requirement to get your business in the black. Only take on those tasks if it aligns with your plans and genuinely enhances your profitability out of desire, not necessity. The business model must stand on its own without requiring you to operate daily for free or at a discounted rate. For further insights on this topic, consider reading *Profit First* by Mike Michalowicz.

Final Thoughts

As I emphasized in Tip #1, knowing your numbers must be the foundation for launching your project. Other than placing my trust in God, knowing my numbers is the only other thing that provides the confidence I need during critical conversations with banks or partners. It's the assurance that I've done my homework and examined every detail. What knowledge will you rely on in those discussions? I do not suggest trying to wing it.

If you find yourself needing assistance with underwriting or evaluating your business plan, I can help. I'm building an online network of real estate focused business owners committed to mutual growth, sharing triumphs and setbacks. Whether you need one-on-one coaching or a business plan review, don't hesitate to reach out. You can find me on all the main social networks.

Lastly, I want to emphasize the importance of your relationships. As Jim Rohn famously said, "You are the average of the five people you spend the most time with."

Reflecting on my journey, I recognize that much of my success can be attributed to the people I surrounded myself with. While having a direct mentor can be invaluable, it's equally important to glean insights from all of the connections you nurture along the way.

ABOUT RYAN MEUER

RYAN MEUER has over two decades of experience in operations. He started his career with a Fortune 500 company, where he quickly rose through the ranks. By the age of 21, he was managing one of the company's largest distribution centers and oversaw a team of over 75 employees. This early success laid the groundwork for his proficiency in handling complex, multifaceted operations.

For the past 17 years, Ryan and his wife have worked together as business owners, building and managing a diverse range of ventures. Their portfolio has included several franchise operations, nightly rental homes, traditional rentals, mobile home parks, RV parks, and self-storage units. Under their leadership, the franchise business grew to generate over $4 million in annual sales across several locations. In 2021, Ryan and his wife decided to focus exclusively on real estate investing, a field they had both been familiar with prior to their business ownership days. They rapidly expanded their real estate holdings to over $8 million in just over two years. Simultaneously, they built a property management company to take care of the day-to-day operations of their properties, as well as others that meet their standards. Their investments include a mix of property types, with The Embers Glamping and RV Resort in Branson Missouri standing out as their most ambitious project—a 14-acre resort built entirely from the ground up.

Ryan continues to apply his expertise in evaluating large-scale projects as he continually grows their real estate portfolio with an expanding network of capital partners. Outside of work, he enjoys family time and organizing remote canoe and backpacking trips, or unwinding with strategic board games.

https://linktr.ee/RyanMeuer

REAL ESTATE INVESTING CHANGED MY LIFE

by Bill Beck

My name is Bill Beck and real estate investing changed my life. I grew up a bit of a nomad and lived in various parts of the Midwest. I knew I always wanted to excel at whatever path I chose in life. My career took a non-linear path working in accounting, credit, quality assurance, entrepreneurship, sales, and finally real estate. Playing "The Game" at various corporations wasn't what I excelled at. I needed to get out of the rat race. Having read *Rich Dad, Poor Dad*, the idea of owning assets and cash flow to replace job income was an epiphany.

In 2017, I started working in a sales role at a nationwide property management company for vacation rentals, *Evolve Vacation Rental*. The sales aspect of the job was very wash-rinse-repeat with identifying pain points and overcoming objections (and other sales buzzwords) on a daily basis. What excited me, though, was the data that I got access to for all of these real estate investors throughout the entire country. I was given a 50,000 ft view of thousands of different vacation rentals and what their results were. One of the first major realizations of the power of investing in this sub asset class was when I created a data set that compared the acquisition price for STR properties and then compared that against what the property actually generated in revenue. Some of the top properties that were operating were purchased in the $200,000 range and making close to $80,000 in Revenue per year. *Insane*. The access to this information prompted me to start a role as a Home Buyer Consultant and to work specifically with investors that wanted to get involved in purchasing this type of property.

I greatly enjoyed learning about various aspects for what makes a successful vacation rental property in the consulting role.

The first major decision to make is: What market do you want to purchase the property in?

In reality, the majority of the United States is not really great for vacation rentals. If you think about it, there are vast swaths of areas that are pretty much entirely rural where not many people are going to. On the opposite end of the spectrum, with major cities they are also a bit of a challenge because they tend to have heavy regulations. Heavy tourism markets have always been the bread and butter for STR investing and the history of occupancy to support investment. Another major consideration is overall occupancy experienced month over month throughout the course of the year.

If an area of the country sees tourism but it's extremely seasonal, for example a town that has a big event for one or two weekends a year but otherwise no major attractions, mountains, beach or lake, it makes it extremely challenging to invest and make it work if the general demand throughout the course of the year is otherwise basically zero.

I helped thousands of buyers with identifying properties and coaching them through the decision-making process for short term rental investing. 2020 was a big year for a lot of people, myself in particular: I purchased my first vacation rental investment in Branson Missouri, the pandemic shut down my office and changed my work dynamic. Nobody was in the position to buy any real estate for a few months. Then real estate came back in one of the most insane feeding frenzies in history. With my background, the choice to relocate to Branson in order to become a real estate agent working with vacation rental investors was a no-brainer.

Having worked both as a vacation rental buyer consultant, and now as a real estate agent working with short-term rental investors, I have a handful of nuggets from experience for anyone that's looking to enter the space. These elements include:

- Revenue to purchase price ratio

- Underwriting for bad management

- Peacocking.

In such a data heavy role one of the first key metrics I look at is a basic ratio.

The Revenue/Purchase Price is very simple and it's essentially the revenue that this property can make in the course of a year divided by the acquisition price. In my experience, if a property isn't able to generate 10% revenue relative to the acquisition price it's generally going to be really difficult to make the property cash flow and generate a return. At around 15% revenue to acquisition price, the deal starts to enter territory where it could make sense.

Anything 20% Revenue/Acquisition Price or higher is generally an incredible opportunity that should be strongly considered.

Bad management is one of the main things that is killing potentially amazing deals. Always factor in comps for similar properties in the area for what true performance potential could be rather than what performance has been for the subject property. Mismanagement can take the form of negligence, bad revenue management strategy, bad boots on the ground, or even simply poor photos and not marketing the property effectively. If you're trying to acquire a high performing property, a seller, "knows what they've got" and is a lot more hesitant to negotiate down on their price. Meanwhile a neighboring property that is pretty similar but has poor historical financials may be an incredible deal if management can be corrected. Property management companies can range in performance across the board but generally the highest performing properties are self managed.

> Always factor in your due diligence on an investment for potential versus historical performance.

One of the standout features of top performing properties I've worked with is they often tend to have a term that I've coined, "Peacocking".

Peacocking is when a property has some element that boldly makes it stand out in photos online when you are marketing it. This can take the form of interior design paint choices, light fixtures, or a specific amenity that nobody else has. When people are browsing through various options to book their experience, having something unique can help you get the booking and have long-term success on the booking algorithm.

> Every single top performing vacation rental I've ever worked with had an element that made it stand out. Always think outside the box on how you can set yourself apart.

I enjoy working with investors and I believe in practicing what I preach. I've assisted a multitude of investors acquire and build portfolios of vacation rental investment properties. I've built my own portfolio of vacation rentals. I have worked close to 200 short term rental transactions since moving to Branson, Missouri and continue to help investors find the best options that are currently available on the market. As I'm currently only licensed for real estate in Missouri, I've decided to branch into other businesses. I've recently partnered with a firm that specializes in mortgage loan origination for vacation rentals primarily in addition to other investment properties. I offer consultation services in addition to real estate and lending.

I found that committing to take action is the first step and the foundation of success. It's imperative to take risks in business. I hope that the information I provided gives some insight into taking more of a calculated risk and to learn from others who have succeeded and from others mistakes.

I want to take a moment to express gratitude to various individuals that have influenced me on my journey.

Special thanks to my parents for everything they've done to support me in this wild life I've lived. Shout out to: Funsho Adesanya, Ryan & Shae Duffy, Lauren Linzer, Melissa Stevens, Adam Sherry, Grant Rotman, Mackenzie Fitzpatrick, Eddie O'Connor, Jeramie & Kelly Worley, Avery Carl, Brenna Carles, Robert Kiyosaki & Amy Hemphill.

About Bill Beck

BILL BECK was born in Missouri and grew up a bit of a nomad, moving all over the Midwest in his youth. He has worked as a business professional for the past 15+ years in disciplines such as accounting, credit, entrepreneurship and real estate investment consulting. Bill saw a major growth and development opportunity while working at a nationwide vacation rental management company. Within the company, he founded the Home Buyer Consulting Division. Bill has personally consulted over 1,000 clients on purchasing over

$100,000,000 worth of STR properties nationwide. He recently re-located to Branson, MO where he has helped hundreds of first time and veteran investors acquire vacation rental assets. He believes in practicing what he preaches and has gone from owning no real estate to owning 4 properties in 4 years. Bill constantly strives to help people achieve their dreams in life through real estate investing and pushing the envelope of what is possible.

Find out more and connect with Bill by visiting the link below.

https://linktr.ee/buywith billbeck

TURN YOUR PROPERTY INTO THE DESTINATION

by Jordan Holmes & Mike Sebastian

Mike and Jordan were on a crash course to meet as they each entered the world of unique short-term rentals. As fate would have it, they did. Shortly after, they began creating incredible unique properties and an education platform for hosts teaching them all the benefits of being unique in a world that doesn't encourage it, called Build Your Hideaway.

Growing up in a small Iowa town, Jordan dreamt of a corporate career, the classic nine-to-five with a nice desk. One conversation during a lunch meeting that he had every intent to skip opened a door to a world he'd never heard of...real estate investing. He quickly became obsessed with the potential financial upside and flexibility it offered him and his family. Fast forward to one year later, he purchased his first short-term rental in Texas. The learning curve was steep. He faced challenges that ranged from breaking up unexpected house parties to communicating with guests during power outages. While not always fun, the experience was invaluable. It didn't take long for Jordan to discover a passion for creating unique guest experiences.With his focus on uniqueness, he discovered three tiny cabins in Kentucky. And, as luck would have it, that was about the same time he met Mike.

Mike, coming from a small town in Virginia, would never have said he had an "entrepreneurial mindset" until after he started his first business in 2015. Looking back, it was obvious it was there all along. At 10 years old, he was mowing lawns for 9 of his neighbors. At 13, he got his first horse and had to generate income to pay for its board. By 24, he'd been working for 14 years as a W2 and was tired of being paid to sit in a seat for a set number of hours each day. Since he worked in marketing, he decided to start a marketing agency and risk leaving the stability of the W2. The next 10 years were a grind, but it worked! After a decade in the marketing world, it was time for a change. He wanted to find something that built more long term wealth. *Enter real estate.*

Every wealthy person Mike talked to had some sort of invest-ment in real estate. It made sense. He decided to leap into the world of real estate by purchasing a single-family home to rent to a family member who needed a nicer place to live. It was safe, and as expected, successful. After that, he acquired another 'safe' short-term rental that had multiple backup options. He launched and it worked! Even better, he ignited a passion for the hospitality side of short-term rentals. His interests grew, and started to venture into treehouses and unique rentals. Here, Mike dove head first into educating himself in this world. That education process led him to Jordan. Together, they learned how to talk with investors, set up deals, acquire more cash flowing properties and quickly acquired 8 more units. *Enter the world of uniqueness.*

Every property they purchased got more unique, and consequently, more profitable. There was a huge barrier to entry that they pushed through without really knowing what was ahead. They started to transform their existing cabins into unique destinations and saw revenues jump by 50% or more with each change. They witnessed firsthand the vast potential that could be unlocked by crafting truly unique properties. It was a perfect blend of their prior skill sets, executed in the STR space. Regardless of your property's location, there are ways to incorporate unique elements into your space. In today's 'attention economy,' standing out is more important than ever. Implement these strategies to create an experience that your guests will find so valuable that they're willing to pay significantly more than your current rates.

Five Perspectives

written by Mike

Over time, we both started to dip our toes into unique properties. First by making standard, boring houses more unique(unique stacking), and then trying out some completely unique builds (unique building). The more unique we got, the more money the rentals produced. But the thing about being unique is that you can't scale easily. Each one has to be one-of-one, or it's not unique by definition. Scaling requires systems. To build a system you have to repeat something over and over again, thus eliminating its uniqueness. Instead, we systematized the research phase into two primary research areas that anyone can use to make their place stand out.

The first research phase covers five different perspectives, or what I like to call lenses, that your unique idea must satisfy in order to continue researching. The process for this is simple. Review your unique idea from top to bottom with each of these lenses on. After you've done it a time or two, you'll be able to complete this exercise in less than 20minutes. Your goal should be to disprove every objection that you find, or identify a failure point and stop with this idea. This is the least expensive point to realize it won't work. Be happy you found it early. There are thousands of ideas out there and as you start researching them, you won't be able to stop thinking about new ones.

The five lenses to use are here:

Lens 1: Thumbstop

Think about whether or not your unique idea will stop a future potential guest, we'll call them FPG's from this point forward, in their scroll. Picture them scrolling past the image of your listing and then pulling back to see it again. It's what I like to call a digital double-take.

The platform the FPG is on doesn't matter. It works the same on Airbnb, as it does VRBO, Instagram, TikTok, and email. Will their first reaction be to stop and dig in more? If so, the thumbstop was a success, move to lens 2.

Lens 2: Emotion

Your idea and the photos that showcase it need to trigger a positive emotion with your FPG. When thinking through your idea with this lens, ask yourself these two questions:

- Can the emotion behind your idea be captured in your listing photos?

- Does this idea increase the positive emotion a guest will feel while visiting?

If your idea shows and delivers emotion, move to lens 3.

Lens 3: Value

Will your target audience find value in your unique idea? If you add a hot tub on top of a cliff that overlooks a beautiful mountainscape, that's something they can share on their social platforms, relaxin, bring friends to, create memories with, etc.

That's valuable to a traveler who is looking to relax and create memories with their friends. For some, a truly unique STR will increase their perceived status amongst friends and family. That's valuable to them AND valuable to you since it's more free exposure. If your idea adds value to your target audience, move to lens 4.

Lens 4: Trust

Does your unique idea build trust with your FPG? Most transactions in the STR space happen without the host and guest actually meeting each other. You have a big hurdle to overcome in building trust with someone before they spend hundreds, or thousands, of dollars to rent your place.

If your place is thought out enough, and looks to be well invested in, it will build trust with those that view it. If you deliver on that when they arrive, the great reviews that come will compound that trust and continue to stack new reservations at your property.

If your idea increases the trust of your FPG, move to lens 5.

Lens 5: Maintenance

This one is typically the quickest to answer, but equally as important. If you're adding on a hot tub, there is maintenance that comes with that. If you're adding a catwalk as an experience that is 3,000' off the ground, you'll need certified people and expensive insurance to operate it. Make sure that the maintenance for your unique idea isn't more costly than the revenue it produces. Also, ensure that the unique idea won't spend more time shut down, or undergoing repairs, thus creating a bad experience for your guests.

Once you've run your idea through these five lenses, you should have a good understanding of how it will grab the attention of your target audience. If you're not 100% confident in the results, keep adjusting your idea, or pivot to a new one altogether. Some of the unique experiences that Jordan and I have put together increased our overall revenue by more than 100%.

> There is a lot of potential in uniqueness
> when you follow this process.

Five Cornerstones to Successful Unique Stays

Written by Jordan

Any investor has the ability to make their property unique, but uniqueness done incorrectly has the potential to financially ruin even a savvy investor. There are critical components you must focus on to ensure your rental is successful. Without them, you're just creating a new headache. We refer to these as our five cornerstones that will help you ensure your property has the highest likelihood to become your market's top-performer.

We'll go through each of them here.

C1. Competitive Analysis

Just because your property will be unique doesn't negate the fact that you must still understand your market inside and out. Start by first understanding the following things about your market:

1. What is the primary reason people travel to your market?

2. What type of people commonly travel to your market?

3. Do the other listings in your market look like they will be hard to beat?

4. How supportive is the local tourism infrastructure?

Focusing on these four things will help you determine the baseline for your unique property. For the first two, we recommend leveraging the power of artificial intelligence, as it can handle larger data-pulls in less time.

From there, you need to understand your market's competition. Competition will be lower if you focus on a market that doesn't have 20,000 other short-term rental properties. Also take into consideration the type of properties available and the perceived skill level of each host.

Lastly, take a look at the current infrastructure within your preferred market. How many grocery stores are open? How many restaurants are there? These items could present long-term challenges for you down the road.

C2. Ideal Guest Persona

Remember, you are not putting this property together for yourself. You are doing so to attract your ideal guest who would travel from anywhere in the country to stay at your place.

You can get a head start on this by identifying the typical visitor to your market today. If you're in downtown Nashville, TN, it's likely a younger visitor traveling there for a concert, bachelor/bachelorette party, or something similar. There's no need to go against the grain here. Expand on this for your unique property.

An example would be a female traveler who is single between the ages 21 to 31 who loves hanging out with her friends. She commonly makes purchasing decisions through social media and happened to find your place while scrolling through Instagram one day. She wants to visit for a girls weekend and see a concert while she's there.

If you can understand your ideal guest, you can then ensure your design, amenities, and marketing efforts align with that ideal guest's interests and desires. This is the secret sauce to maximize your property's revenue potential.

Remember, guests that don't fit this persona can still book your place, but 100% of your design and marketing decisions should be geared towards this one guest avatar.

C3. Consistency from Design to Implementation

It must be seamless. Every part must flow together. This is where details truly matter. We've received hundreds of compliments and reviews that state "You thought of everything."

Make sure you think of everything.

This doesn't mean you need to do it alone, hiring a designer is money well spent. They know how to take your blank slate and turn it into a design masterpiece. Encourage the designer to be bold here. Find different ways to allow you space to stand out or "pop". Murals do a fantastic job of this. Bonus points if you can sprinkle in local components to make it truly one-of-one. Complement this with amenities done uniquely, while still maintaining the consistency of your space. If you can spark an excited, positive emotion in your guests the moment they get out of their car and then maintain that for the duration of their trip, you have just culminated a recipe for maximum repeat guests.

C4. Financing Unique Projects

The fact that your property is unique means finding comps for conventional financing can be challenging. This may result in appraisals coming in lower than expected. Not a deal breaker, but something you need to be aware of heading into it.

When talking with banks or lenders, choose your terminology carefully. The term "unique" with banks may raise a red flag as banks typically prefer lots of data to prove it will be stable and reliable for them to minimize the risk. Consider explaining your project to them in the simplest terms without explaining how unique and one-of-a-kind it will be - no matter how excited you are.

Bankers love knowing that you've done this before. Share your work history and prior successes with them up front so they know you have experience with this type of project.

Bonus points if you can meet the banker in person and show them your lot and highlight your experience in the space.

C5.Strategic Marketing

You can and will gain traction from Airbnb and VRBO by simply being unique. But relying on these platforms to promote your property puts you in the same category as everyone else who is playing the "algorithm game." This is not unique and will not maximize your revenue.

First, start by differentiating your listing photos. There are three tiers of listing photos, iPhone photos, real estate photos, and short-term rental photos. Go with the third option. STR photographers know how to capture your property in a way that will stand out.

There is so much untapped potential on social platforms like Instagram and TikTok. Create accounts on both platforms and structure each like their very own listing. Then work with a short-term rental videographer to capture your property from a unique lens. Take that content and curate exciting, engaging videos to promote your unique place to thousands and even millions of potential guests, for free!

Lastly, leverage your email list. If you have hosted for any amount of time, you already have a list of emails from your past guests. Communicate with them!

For advanced users, you can implement email capture solutions in your property to collect emails for each guest when they log in to your internet. Use that list to send weekly emails encouraging them to come back for years to come. Don't expect an overnight rush from this. It takes a while, but is very high ROI if you're consistent.

Call To Action

We've created a ton of resources to train hosts how to do all of this. It's created to meet hosts where they are in their hosting journey today, whether that's just getting started or adding their 100th unit.

Some are free and some are not. If you're serious about making your next project unique, learn more here:

http://buildyourhideaway.com/fearlessfoundations

Conclusion

As we close out this chapter, you should have a deep understanding of where our drive comes from, the road we took to get here, as well as the reason we continue to work in this space.

None of this would be possible without the love and support of our spouses, Courtney and Allie. It's not easy hearing, "I'm driving to [INSERT RANDOM CITY NAME HERE]" as frequently as we have both had to say it, but both Courtney and Allie have relentlessly encouraged our curiosity and drive, and sometimes even our insanity.

Secondarily we'd like to thank our mentors, partners, and investors that trusted us with their time and money. We were once inexperienced and ignorant, but always driven. These individuals trusted us with their most valuable assets, time and money, enabling us to get where we are today.

Don't stop being curious. The best ideas for unique builds are the ones that sound impossible at first.

Keep digging, keep asking, and keep adjusting until you find the one that works. Then hold on tight and make sure your systems are dialed in, because your inbox will overwhelm you with new reservations.

We have a team of on-site managers, cleaners, realtors, builders, handymen, landscapers, lenders, investors, therapists and more that make this entire journey possible. Without them, none of this would work.

A chain is only as strong as its weakest link, and the team that holds us together is no different.

ABOUT JORDAN HOLMES & MIKE SEBASTIAN

JORDAN HOLMES is an Iowa-based real estate investor known for his talent to transform properties into extraordinary guest experiences. His journey into real estate began unexpectedly, sparked by a casual conversation that ignited a passion for the industry of real estate investing. Like many new investors, Jordan explored various avenues before settling on short-term rentals – specifically unique short-term rentals.

His initial venture, a beach house in Crystal Beach, Texas, while promising, ultimately fell short of expectations. This setback led him to discover an up-and-coming market in the Red River Gorge located in the great state of Kentucky. A turning point came with a connection to fellow investor Mike Sebastian through a short-term rental mastermind group. Their shared vision for creating exceptional guest experiences through uniquely designed and crafted properties made them a great team. Together, they've built a portfolio of unique properties in the Red River Gorge and Hocking Hills, Ohio.

What Jordan and Mike have learned is that maximizing revenue often depends on building a truly distinctive property. As guest expectations rise, differentiation becomes crucial. Their properties are designed to be destinations in themselves, offering unparalleled experiences. They have also realized the untapped marketing potential through social media platforms like Instagram and TikTok. Their marketing strategies have yielded millions of organic impressions resulting in a substantial increase for their percentage of direct bookings.

Beyond their investment portfolio, Holmes and Sebastian are committed to sharing their expertise. Through mentorship and education, they empower aspiring investors to thrive in the unique short-term rental and hospitality industry by crafting properties that captivate guests. Their focus on innovative design, exceptional amenities, and strategic marketing has yielded impressive results. By demystifying the complexities of the short-term rental market and providing actionable strategies, Holmes and Sebastian help investors turn their real estate dreams into reality.

MIKE SEBASTIAN is a real estate investor and entrepreneur with a diverse background. Born and raised in Richmond, Virginia, his adventurous spirit led him to live in different parts of the country, including San Diego, Seattle, and Louisville. His journey into real estate started in 2020 when he bought his first rental property. After dipping his toes in that world, armed with a decade of experience building and scaling a digital marketing agency, Mike realized a gap in the short-term rental market and decided to make the jump to work there full time.

Mike quickly assembled a portfolio of 16 properties, focusing primarily on short-term rentals. His automation-driven approach allowed him to optimize performance and maximize returns quickly. A chance encounter with Jordan Holmes in a real estate mastermind group proved to be a pivotal moment, as their complementary skill sets formed the foundation of a successful partnership.

While Mike's portfolio spans various markets, he has developed a particular affinity for the Red River Gorge in eastern Kentucky. This region's natural beauty and growing popularity as a tourist destination aligned perfectly with his vision for creating exceptional guest experiences. Beyond real estate, Mike is an avid skydiver with over 650 jumps under his belt. He also enjoys the simple pleasures of riding horses, hiking, and hosting at-home BBQs.

Mike's journey from digital marketing to real estate investing is a testament to his entrepreneurial spirit and adaptability. His passion for creating unique rental properties, combined with his business acumen, has positioned him well in the industry.

*https://buildyourhideaway.c
om/linktree*

Real Estate Investing Strategies for Success

by Vinci Sevilla Jr.

My wife and I have grown our business from 8 short term rentals to over 100+ short term rental listings in less than a year using the exact strategy and systems I explain in detail below. Our portfolio has expanded across 7 states and includes a 40-acre campground resort, two boutique hotels, and a 550 acre ranch where 330 acres is a dedicated animal safari reserve. We have incorporated four main sources of revenue from each property:

1. **Accommodations / Lodging:** providing some of the most unique stays and amenities in the entire world

2. **Events**: hosting weddings, corporate events or retreats at our beautiful venues.

3. **Upsells**: activities and experiences like ATVs, pontoon boats, kayaks, horse-back riding, safari tours, etc. We have built the attractions that bring in our guests.

4. **Food & Beverage**: we have built on-site restaurants and food services that cater to our guests and offer special packages for our events.

The section below is an introduction to property management at scale for small to large portfolios anywhere from single short term rentals to large commercial properties like campgrounds and glamping resorts. While one of the main challenges is the hands-on nature of managing these assets, I believe that leveraging technology and building the right systems can elevate guest experiences and streamline operations, enabling you to work from anywhere in the world.

Getaway Haus is the nation's premier property management company that specializes in managing luxury short term rentals, hotels, campgrounds, and resorts.

Introduction to Property Management and Operations

Property management and operations encompass the strategies, processes, and responsibilities involved in overseeing and maintaining rental properties. In the context of short-term rentals, campgrounds, and glamping resorts, property management extends beyond standard tasks to include delivering memorable guest experiences, optimizing resources, and maintaining high operational standards. A well-run property management system ensures that each guest's stay is seamless, with clean accommodations, responsive service, and engaging amenities. Campgrounds and glamping sites in particular face the added challenge of providing rustic charm while maintaining safety, cleanliness, and modern conveniences, all of which require careful management.

This sector also presents unique challenges and opportunities. Seasonal demand, environmental considerations, and the maintenance of remote or nature-focused locations add complexity to day-to-day operations. However, with thoughtful planning and the adoption of technology like property management software and automation, these challenges can become opportunities to stand out.

For those willing to innovate, the rewards are significant: the chance to build a high-performing, profitable operation while providing unforgettable experiences that keep guests returning year after year.

Automate your Operations using Tech integrations and AI

Automation and AI are revolutionizing property management for short-term rentals, campgrounds, and glamping resorts, making daily operations more efficient while enhancing guest satisfaction. Through the use of Property Management Systems (PMS), online booking platforms, and smart technologies, property managers can streamline check-ins, manage amenities, and provide personalized services that elevate the guest experience.

Daily Operations and Workflow

Automated tools enable smoother daily operations such as check-in and check-out procedures through smart locks or mobile apps, eliminating the need for staff at arrival and departure times. Property management systems (PMS) streamline scheduling, maintenance requests, and housekeeping updates, keeping everything in sync. Automated housekeeping reminders help maintain cleanliness standards, while smart sensors can track room occupancy, notifying staff when spaces are ready for cleaning.

Managing Amenities and Safety Protocols

Amenities like pools, recreational areas, and communal kitchens can be managed through IoT devices, which monitor usage, water levels, and maintenance needs. Automation also supports emergency protocols, with AI-driven systems capable of detecting unusual activity or hazards, allowing quick responses to ensure guest safety.

Enhancing Guest Experience and Personalization

Personalized guest services elevate the experience and AI can capture guest preferences, such as room types, specific accommodations, or activities, to tailor future stays. Automated upsells for activities or events can be sent directly to guests' mobile devices, offering relevant experiences that enhance their trip while boosting revenue.

Handling Guest Feedback

AI tools are invaluable in analyzing guest feedback in real-time. By gauging sentiment in guest communications AI can detect dissatisfaction early, prompting staff to resolve issues before they escalate. This proactive approach can prevent negative reviews, helping maintain high ratings and guest loyalty.

Customer Loyalty Programs

With automated loyalty programs, guests are encouraged to return or refer friends. AI can offer discounts for future stays, giftable vouchers, or referral incentives, boosting repeat business and brand loyalty.

Smart Technology for Convenience

Smart technologies like automated climate control, lighting, and virtual assistants offer added convenience. By integrating these features, property managers can provide a modern, comfortable environment that enhances guests' overall experience.

By incorporating automation and AI, property managers can elevate operations, drive guest satisfaction, and enhance efficiency, making these technologies essential for managing successful short-term rentals and glamping resorts.

Building a Remote Team: Step-by-Step Guide to Scale Efficiently

Building and scaling a remote team for property management allows you to access a global talent pool, reduce overhead, and create a highly adaptable team to support your growing operations.

Here's a step-by-step approach to build and expand your remote team effectively:

Step 1: Define the Roles You Need

Begin by identifying the specific roles required for your operation. For property management in the short-term rental or glamping sector, you'll want a blend of administrative support, customer service, and operational oversight. Start small, focusing initially on hiring a general virtual assistant (VA) who can grow with your business. This VA should handle basic tasks such as guest inquiries, booking management, and administrative support, allowing you to focus on growth.

Actionable Step: Write detailed job descriptions for each role you foresee needing, even if you aren't hiring for them immediately. Include primary responsibilities, expected outcomes, and essential skills. This foundation will make scaling smoother as you begin to add more roles.

Step 2: Recruit and Hire Virtual Assistants (VAs)

With a job description in hand, start the recruitment process. Online platforms like Upwork, OnlineJobs.ph, Facebook or LinkedIn can help you find skilled VAs from around the world. When interviewing, focus on candidates' communication skills, time management, and problem-solving abilities, as these qualities are critical for remote work.

Actionable Step: Develop a structured interview process that includes a mix of behavioral and situational questions. Also provide a small test task to evaluate their practical skills in real-world scenarios. One thing I make every candidate do is take a personality test, one that typically follows the DISC personality assessment.

Step 3: Start with an Executive Assistant

Your first hire should be a versatile executive assistant who can handle a variety of tasks and grow into a leadership role. This individual will ideally become your operations manager as your business expands. In addition to handling daily tasks, train this person to take on hiring, onboarding, and managing new VAs over time.

Actionable Step: Create a training program for your executive assistant. Start with shadowing sessions to demonstrate key processes, then gradually assign more complex responsibilities. Offer feedback regularly to ensure their development aligns with your operational goals.

Step 4: Establish Clear Communication and Workflow Tools

Remote teams thrive with structured communication and task management systems. Use tools like Slack for daily communication, Asana or Trello for task management, and Google Drive or Dropbox for document storage. Setting up these systems will keep your team organized and allow them to collaborate efficiently from anywhere. Project management tools such as Monday.com, Airtable, and Notion are great ways to keep things organized.

Actionable Step: Set up a shared calendar and establish regular check-in meetings, either weekly or bi-weekly. Clearly outline expectations for communication, such as response times and update frequencies, so everyone stays aligned.

Step 5: Create Standard Operating Procedures (SOPs) and Training Materials

Standard operating procedures (SOPs) and training materials are crucial for maintaining consistency and quality across a remote team. Documenting your processes allows for smooth onboarding and scalability. Use written documents, video tutorials, or screen recordings to create a training library.

Actionable Step: Start by creating SOPs for essential tasks (e.g., guest check-in procedures, issue escalation). As your executive assistant gains experience, they can help refine and expand these documents.

Step 6: Build a Retention Strategy for Remote Employees

To retain skilled remote employees, provide competitive compensation, flexible schedules, and opportunities for professional development. Recognize achievements and maintain regular contact to build loyalty and engagement. Since many remote workers value flexibility, consider offering options like performance bonuses or paid time off.

Actionable Step: Set up a monthly one-on-one with each team member to discuss their goals, performance, and any feedback. This helps foster a supportive work environment and ensures employees feel valued.

Step 7: Manage On-Site Staff as Needed

For campgrounds and glamping resorts, you'll need reliable on-site staff like cleaners and maintenance workers. Invest time in hiring skilled local staff to maintain property standards, as their work directly impacts guest satisfaction. Build connections with local providers to ensure you have dependable resources, especially during peak seasons.

Actionable Step: Develop a system for coordinating between your remote team and on-site staff. Assign your executive assistant or a VA to handle communication with on-site staff, ensuring timely updates and issue reporting.

Step 8: Scale Strategically

As your operations grow, gradually add specialized roles to your remote team. Consider bringing on VAs with expertise in guest relations, marketing, and data analytics. Empower your executive assistant to lead this hiring process, following the initial framework you created.

Actionable Step: Set milestones to evaluate when it's time to add roles. For example, when guest inquiries reach a certain volume, it may be time to hire a guest relations assistant.

By following these steps, you can build a robust, scalable remote team for property management that supports your growth, minimizes costs, and enhances your ability to provide exceptional guest experiences.

Future Trends in Glamping
and Campground Management

The glamping and campground industry is thriving, with travelers increasingly seeking nature-connected experiences that offer modern conveniences. Embracing future trends and technologies can help properties meet these demands while opening new revenue streams.

Here's a look at some key trends, along with actionable steps to help implement them.

- **Hosting Weddings and Corporate Events:** Hosting weddings and corporate events can be highly lucrative, especially if your property has scenic spaces suitable for gatherings. Start by identifying areas that could serve as outdoor or semi-outdoor venues and work on creating a flexible event space that can be easily transformed. Ensure essential infrastructure like electricity, restroom facilities, and accessible pathways are in place. Partnering with local wedding planners or event organizers can help generate initial bookings. Develop event packages that cater to different budgets, and consider including perks like discounted accommodations for guests attending the events.

- **Food and Beverage Concepts:** Adding a food and beverage option provides guests with an all-in-one experience, encouraging them to stay longer. Start by assessing guest demand and available space for a café, bar, or small restaurant. If you're not ready to commit to a full-service kitchen, consider options like food trucks, pop-up vendors, or a partnership with local caterers to offer pre-made meals. Seasonal locally-sourced ingredients will not only cut costs but also add an authentic regional feel to your offerings which guests love.

- **General Store or Mercantile Shop:** A general store or mercantile shop can provide guests with essentials, snacks, and souvenirs while boosting revenue. Begin by curating a small selection of local goods, snacks, and camping essentials. A well-stocked general store with branded merchandise, local crafts, and travel necessities can increase convenience and enhance the guest experience. Use a point-of-sale (POS) system to track inventory, and focus on high-margin items like souvenirs and branded gear.

- **Predictions for Industry Growth and Opportunities:** As demand for outdoor, eco-friendly getaways continues to rise, properties that combine luxury with sustainability and unique offerings will likely see long-term success. Consider expanding wellness amenities to tap into the trend of health-focused travel, like adding yoga decks, meditation areas, or spa services. Properties that cater to digital nomads might offer extended stay options with high-speed Wi-Fi, dedicated workspaces, and comfortable amenities for remote work. Sustainable practices and smart technology are leading trends in glamping. Incorporating green features like solar panels, rainwater systems, and energy-efficient appliances not only reduces environmental impact but also appeals to eco-conscious guests. To get started, consider conducting an energy audit to assess your property's sustainability needs, then phase in eco-friendly upgrades that are affordable and impactful.

Actionable Tips for Growth and Expansion

1. Start Small with Add-ons: Introduce basic offerings like event packages or a small café. Gradually scale up based on guest feedback and profitability.

2. Partner with Local Vendors: Work with local suppliers for food, retail, and event services to support regional businesses and save on logistics.

3. Trial Programs for New Services: Test new amenities—such as yoga sessions, guided nature walks, or glamping tents—on a short-term basis. Gather feedback to see if these services appeal to your audience.

4. Promote Unique Experiences Online: Invest in digital marketing to showcase unique offerings, like scenic weddings,

sustainable practices, or specialized retreats. Use online booking platforms to increase visibility and drive engagement. Partnering with social media influencers by offering incentives like a discounted or free night stay has helped widen our own audience and guest outreach.

With these trends and actionable steps, glamping and campground managers can successfully implement new ideas, enhancing the guest experience and driving additional revenue while staying on top of the industry's growth trajectory.

Scaling Your Property Management & Operations

As you look to grow your glamping resort or campground, here are some practical steps based on key principles we've covered, all geared toward helping you create a scalable, well-managed, and profitable business.

- **Automate Essential Operations**: Use Property Management Systems (PMS) and AI-driven tools to automate tasks like booking, check-in/out, and guest communication. This reduces manual workload and allows your team to focus on providing exceptional service. Start by evaluating different PMS platforms to find one that fits your property size and needs.

- **Develop a Consistent Workflow**: Establish standard operating procedures (SOPs) for daily tasks, from housekeeping to guest check-ins. These can be documented in a manual or digital format accessible to all staff. SOPs ensure that, as you scale, each guest receives a consistent, high-quality experience, regardless of team size.

- **Diversify Revenue Streams**: Add additional services and experiences, like weddings, corporate retreats, or wellness activities, which can be scheduled during low seasons to increase occupancy. Start small—consider offering weekend yoga retreats or partner with local event organizers to test the demand for events on your property.

- **Leverage Upselling and Loyalty Programs**: Use automated upsells to encourage guests to add activities or amenities during their stay. Additionally, launch a loyalty program that offers discounts for returning guests or referrals. Consider offering seasonal discounts, birthday specials, or a referral discount that can entice guests to return or refer friends.

- **Invest in Staff Training and Retention**: As your business grows, having well-trained staff is essential. Create onboarding and training programs that teach staff everything from operations to guest interaction, making it easier to scale while maintaining quality. Consider using online training tools to keep everyone aligned with your service standards.

- **Stay Adaptable and Open to Feedback**: Scaling requires flexibility. Gather guest feedback after every stay to understand what's working and where you can improve. Use surveys, review analysis, or AI sentiment tools to gauge satisfaction. Being proactive in addressing feedback builds loyalty and helps refine your offerings.

By taking these actionable steps, you can effectively scale your glamping property, creating a streamlined, guest-focused operation that is both sustainable and profitable. Each improvement will help set your business up for long-term success in a competitive and evolving market.

About Vinci Sevilla Jr.

'You miss 100% of the shots you don't take. -Wayne Gret-zky'–Michael Scott"

VINCI SEVILLA JR. is a proud husband and father and an active real estate investor and entrepreneur. He holds a portfolio valued in excess of $35M consisting of long term rentals, short term vacation rentals, and large multi-families. Vinci is the Founder and CEO of Getaway Haus, a technology and data driven real estate investment and management firm. Their national portfolio specializes in managing and operating top tier vacation short term rentals, hotels, campgrounds, and resorts and are actively expanding across the U.S. Vinci is also the Co-Founder of NVST Capital, where they take on large multifamily syndications and help investors maximize their returns.

Vinci is a seasoned keynote speaker and thought leader in promoting financial independence and real estate investing. He is a best-selling author and has written and co-authored on topics such as short term rentals (Hospitable Hosts vol 2) and the power of partnerships (Real Estate Partnerships by Bigger Pockets). Vinci is also active in establishing local real estate investing communities and hosts his own real estate meet-ups where building wealth and financial freedom are at the core.

Vinci's greatest accomplishment and his WHY is his family. He and his wife, Patricia, were barely 5 months pregnant when they began setting up their first short term rental. They could never have imagined how much this journey would transform their lives.

https://linktr.ee/vinci_sevilla_jr

LEVERAGING FOR WEALTH

by Ryan Duffy

Leverage the hidden value within your land to create wealth in ways you may have never considered. Through creative land planning, lot line separations, tax incentives, and equity partnerships, take your business to the next level and start thinking beyond individual properties.

I will share the following case studies:

- How a lot line separation turned a dilapidated garage into a $100,000 land parcel and a STR generating unbelievable cash on cash returns.

- How we turned a dilapidated house surrounded by old trailers into a micro resort valued at $1,500,000 that we own 33% of with only $5,160 of our own money.

- How we turned 23 acres of raw land into a one of a kind STR subdivision with the help of partners to generate over $400,000 of profit in just over 12 months.

From my experience as a real estate broker assisting hosts to buy and sell investment properties, I've seen first hand how difficult it has become over the past couple of years to find options that have the potential to cash flow. My goal is to educate others on the value of new construction and land development to create amazing destinations rather than relying solely on existing inventory.

> You don't need a lot of money to be a developer, you need a vision and the guts to pursue it.

You can create the team you need to build unique, custom stays.

$100k for a Dilapidated Garage

In December of 2021, my wife Shae and I purchased our third investment property. We had just sold a home that we had renovated with partners and set up as a short term rental and utilized a 1031 exchange to acquire an off market three bed three bath on an acre and a half with a detached garage. The property needed a lot of work but we could see tremendous potential. We made great money flipping our previous two properties and felt that the return on this one would be the best yet.

Our niche is custom one of a kind short term rental properties. We operate in an area that has become oversaturated with cookie cutter homes that are crowded into resort-like communities.

Converting homes on larger pieces of land into short term rentals in our market gives us the ability to acquire properties that tend to perform better than the competition at a lower acquisition price and a much faster return on equity. They outperform most other like sized properties and tend to have a lower operating expense (no HOA, COA or commercial tax valuation in our case).

We purchased this particular home for $190,000 putting down $120,000 with our 1031 exchange. It appraised as is for $200,000 at the time of purchase.

We were able to pull a line of credit to cover most of the extensive remodel which came out to about $150,000. We removed load bearing walls and replaced them with engineered beams to open up the living spaces. We added a fourth bedroom and bathroom and transformed the outdoor space.

At this point, we were all into the property for $340,000. We owed $220,000 on the debt service and the after renovation appraisal came back at $425,000 in the summer of 2021. The Emerald Escape was now an active short term rental property and generating great returns.

In its first consecutive twelve months of operations, it grossed $82,000 with us blocking off approximately six weeks for personal use. *What about the garage?*

One of the first thoughts was to demolish it. It was built on a great foundation but the structure itself was falling apart. If it stood a little closer to the main house, it would have been great to repurpose into a game room. Having a garage doesn't do a whole lot to add value to a short term rental property.

At this point in time, our careers seemed to be taking off. We were busier than we had ever been as a real estate brokerage and the construction side of our business was growing rapidly. Shae's parents had been a godsend for us. They helped with the kids pretty much every weekend (and many week nights) so that we could work our crazy schedules. To say thank you, we gave them the garage.

We wanted to help them establish an investment property for themselves. They had equity in their personal home, so we suggested that they take out a home equity line of credit and use it to rebuild the garage into a tiny home rental that we would manage for them.

We operate in an area that is not subject to any planning and zoning restrictions. We are outside of city limits and the state of Arkansas will allow you to do a lot line separation on your property without going through a subdivision review process in some instances. We hired a surveyor, marked off a half acre for the garage to sit on and turned it into its own parcel. We hooked it up to municipal water, added a septic system, and rebuilt it from the foundation up to create a 440 square foot studio cabin that we call the Pearl Bay.

Total construction cost: $90,000
Appraised value: $209,000
First year revenue: $50,000

The appraisal was not income based. It was performed immediately after construction to be able to mortgage the property and repay the line of credit that was used for construction. It gave a $100,000 valuation to the half acre lake view lot that was created when we separated the garage from the larger property. This did nothing to diminish the value of the main house.

In the fall of 2023, we sold the Emerald Escape for $625,000.

The Pearl Bay is still owned by our family and remains one of the highest performing units we manage from an NOI perspective.

If We Had the Money

In October of 2022, a six acre property came up for sale on my street that had a house and three single wide trailers on it. It was listed for $185,000. I put an offer on it with an assignable contract and started trying to figure out what to do with it. The property was rough but I loved the location. It was close to several major tourist draws with no restrictions.

We had just started working with some friends who wanted to get into the short term rental space. In one of our initial conversations, I had an Ah Ha moment. We were openly discussing how well our other short term rental properties have performed over the years. We were asked an interesting question.

"If these really do so well, why don't you own ten of them?"

My response was, "We don't have a million dollars in the bank."

Her response shifted my mindset, "So your only limitation is capital?"

Capital

Many of us find ourselves stuck in a poverty mindset. We focus too much on the limitations that keep us from growing our businesses. Until this conversation, Shae and I never really considered the option of bringing on partners. We didn't want to share ownership of a property. The idea seemed daunting. What if the partnership didn't work out? What if we failed to perform up to our partners' expectations? What we had been doing for the past few years seemed to be working well but we were limited by our own personal capital and our own borrowing power.

Our friends presented us with the idea of a joint venture. If Shae and I came up with the design concept, executed the build out at cost (in lieu of a general contractor fee), and built the management structure to handle operations, they would back the construction loan and put up the money for the down payment. We would all evenly contribute to the initial down payment for the property purchase.

Our third of that contribution came out to $5,160, slightly less than the commission I received for my buyers agency commission.

The partnership we went on to form consists of Shae, myself, and two other couples. The operating agreement along with the memorandum of understanding for the new LLC clearly outlined each partners' respective contributions, expectations, and responsibilities. Once the LLC was incorporated, we assigned the sales contract to the new entity and moved forward with the closing. Through inspections, we were able to secure some seller concessions and bring the sales price down to $175,000.

The build out was budgeted for $1,200,000 to create four high end cabins spread across the six acre property. Each cabin would be fully furnished and equipped with private hot tubs, steam showers, and observation decks to view the stars at night. They would share a heated indoor pool, additional hot tub, workout facility, and outdoor firepit.

When we purchased the property, it consisted of a four bedroom house and three single wide mobile homes. All of the structures were in a significant state of disrepair but were occupied by long term month to month tenants. The mobiles had leaky roofs, broken windows, and rotten subfloors. The house wasn't much better. Once the properties were vacated, we had to raze the structures but wanted to find a way to put them to use before we started hauling them off.

I reached out to local police and fire departments to see if there was any interest in using the property as a training ground for first responders prior to demolition. I spent nine years as a firefighter prior to starting my real estate career and remembered the value of being able to simulate real world situations in a training environment. Unfortunately, Arkansas Department of

Natural Resources rules won't allow for live burn exercises, so I couldn't get any of the local fire departments to participate. The SWAT team from a neighboring police department was down to train though.

For almost two weeks, they worked their way through the house and three mobiles. They simulated hostage negotiation drills, forced entry, and clearing rooms. They shot charges and broke every window. They breached every door with battering rams. They shot out the locks, broke down the walls, and even threw CS gas (tear gas) through the windows. By the time they were done, every structure on the property was thoroughly destroyed and no longer habitable.

Prior to the drill, we had every participant sign a liability waiver and even emailed with the captain to see if they would be willing to sign off on a charitable donation receipt. After all, despite the poor condition of these homes at the time of purchase, they were still habitable prior to this training exercise. We had to put a valuation on the charitable donation of the structures.

The simplest way was to pull from the appraisal. According to the appraiser, the value of the improvements on the land at the time of purchase came out to $120,000. Our accountant instructed us to have the appraiser sign off on an IRS form 8283 for Noncash Charitable Contributions.

We were able to write off the $120,000 as a charitable donation and give local first responders a rare training opportunity prior to starting our project.

We call the development the Constellations at Table Rock Lake. It is a high end couples only destination that is located near a new concert venue, wedding destination, and a full service marina on Table Rock Lake near Branson, Missouri. It is unlike any other short term rental development in the area and is on track to perform very well. It was a tremendous amount of work, but I think the payout will be worth it.

We hold exclusive management rights to the property at 15% of total revenue along with a third of the equity. Our conservative proformas have the development grossing approximately $240,000 per year.

Phase one of the development was completed in August 2024 with the first four cabins going into service. The indoor heated pool was completed in October and initial bookings have been coming in at the rates and occupancy we had forecasted.

Phase two will be to leverage the increased equity and cash flow to build an additional four to six glamping units on the property.

Creating Inventory

Early spring of 2023, we noticed a market demand that was not being filled. Our brokerage was working with hundreds of investors looking to purchase short term rental properties but there were few good options to sell them. The heyday of the post-Covid short term rental boom was winding down. Purchase prices were still up and occupancy numbers were starting to drop down to more normalized levels. It was becoming harder and harder to find options that had a high potential for cash flow. Most of what was available in our market consisted of older condos and over-built cookie cutter lodges.

We had our eye on what seemed like a great spot to develop.

Buy Dirt

Twenty three acres had come up for sale along Cricket Creek

where it feeds into Table Rock Lake. It consisted of two separate parcels. Thirteen acres where an old house had burned down years ago on the north side of the road and another ten acre parcel on the south side fronting the creek. The southern ten acres laid relatively flat and seemed to have little rock. Two features that are rare in our geographic area.

One of the biggest initial expenses associated with a housing development is infrastructure. If you have to hire a rock breaker to assist in the installation of your underground services (water and power) you're looking at a major wildcard expense. It's typically in the area of $180 per hour and you may not know if it will take eight hours to complete the job or two months.

The creek front acreage was lightly wooded and easily walkable to not just the creek, but the lake itself. It seemed like an excellent location to build some small cabins in the woods. We put together a plan to subdivide and sell ten one acre lots on that parcel. The proceeds from the lot sales would more than pay for the entire twenty three acre land acquisition. We would then have the remaining 13 acres to sell or develop for ourselves.

We had never subdivided property before. We had success with smaller lot line separations but this was a little bit of a different animal. We researched the process and started assessing the viability of the project.

One of the reasons why this parcel looked appealing from a development perspective, other than location to major attractions and natural amenities, is that it fell outside of any planning and zoning restrictions. There were no limitations on the use of the property for short term renal activity. This helped simplify the subdivision process for us. There was no municipal or county authority to deal with, only the state of Arkansas.

The state required that a proposed subdivision be surveyed out to show the new lot lines and have sanitation requirements engineered into each lot prior to state approval. We also had to confirm the source of water for the build sites and access to electricity. Much of this we would have to do after closing on the property.

At the time this opportunity presented itself, we did not have the liquidity to take on another project. We were just wrapping up the build for our personal home and a custom shipping container home. Both projects have been very capital intensive. We were determined to find a way to make it work though. We offered the property with a long escrow period contingent on satisfactory surveys and financing. The seller accepted and we went to work trying to figure out how to buy it.

The contract price was $286,000 for the twenty three acre property.

We had pre-approval for a six month interest only land loan if we could come up with 30% to put down on the purchase, $85,800.

I shared my plan with everyone I could think of who may have an interest or potentially know someone who would potentially invest in the idea. A couple of our good friends and colleagues decided to take the calculated risk with us and we were able to proceed. They pulled a home equity line of credit and offered to put the money down for the land loan. We would co-sign on the note and share the profits after repaying their HELOC contribution and any other expenses associated with the build out.

We had a few other considerations to take into account as we started working through our diligence period and moved towards closing. We were actively working to line up potential buyers and we were starting to get some feedback on the location.

The property was only accessible by a dirt road. My rebuttal was that it's a county maintained dirt road and it's not very far off of the pavement. I felt that it would actually prove to be an endearing feature for a vacation rental development. After all, we vacationed in the area for years from Chicago before deciding to relocate permanently. When we reached the dirt road, we knew we were almost there and it was time for our vacation to officially begin.

The property sits at the bottom of a valley and has very limited cell phone reception. Several potential investors commented that they felt this could make the properties hard to sell and difficult to rent. There was an easy fix to this one. We made the issue clear to all of our prospective buyers and suggested that they plan on installing cell phone signal boosters.

The biggest potential hurdle was determining that a good amount of the property fell under a flowage easement from the Army Corps of Engineers.

Table Rock Lake is an Army Corps controlled lake. When they built the lake back in the 1950s, the Corps established what they call flowage easements along many of the creeks and tributaries that feed into it. The property these easements set on are privately owned, but no one is allowed to build any structures or change the topography in such a way that could impact the flow of water into the lake.

Full consideration of potential contingencies is imperative in real estate deals. Our survey contingency is what stood to protect us in the event that we determined the location of this flowage easement would be a detriment to development potential.

Each of the one acre lots bordered the creek. This is what made them attractive. We could clear out little build sites in the woods and each could have a private trail to the water. The location also raised some concern from buyers and lenders. Is it set in a flood plain? Would owners be required to maintain flood insurance?

The flowage easement was tied to a specific elevation, 936 feet above sea level. This was the highest mark the Corps of Engineers could flood the lake to. It would also put the land along that easement under water. According to the insurance companies, the fact that each of these new lots had a portion of this easement across them meant that they were subject to a low risk flood rating. However, since the flood zone only applied to the actual area affected by the easement and we were not permitted to build on it, the flood insurance could be dropped by getting an updated survey after the home is built to demonstrate that none of it was touching the flood zone.

When the results from the topographical survey came back, we were pleasantly surprised. There was actually a good deal more space outside of the flowage easement than the estimates provided to us from the Corps showed. We were able to determine that there was enough buildable space on the acreage to layout a small subdivision that would be financially viable. We closed on the property and began working through the rest of the process.

We determined in our early diligence that we had room for ten one acre lots. We drew it out using satellite overlays (Google Earth) for approximate distances and then went out with a measuring wheel and marking paint to lay out the general dimensions. Once we were satisfied with where everything laid out, we brought our surveyors back out to mark the corners and modify our distances as needed to make sure each parcel came out to an even acre.

The next step was to design and engineer the actual subdivision. In hindsight, we should have started this portion prior to closing on the property to confirm viability of the project. I'll get more into that at the end. The two biggest considerations to a state subdivision approval are access to potable water and sewer plan. Here in rural Arkansas, and much of the Ozarks, we rely on private wells and septic systems.

Proper design of your waste disposal starts with where your water is coming from. If you have a well on or near the property, you have to keep all septic components a minimum of one hundred feet away from the wellhead. This is a limiting factor when laying out your subdivision. Lots that require private or shared wells typically have to be larger to accommodate this set back.

Fortunately for us, there was a rural water service line that ended just 3000 feet from the property we were looking to develop. We contacted the water department when we were first doing our due diligence on the property to verify if that was an option for us to tie in to. They confirmed it was and sent us an email stating that they would be willing to support the development.

The fact that our lots had access to public water meant we didn't have to worry about the setback.

The next major consideration to a subdivision plan is sanitation. For our project, just ten small homes, it didn't make sense to consider a sewer plant. That would have been cost prohibitive as they typically start around $250k in our area. Individual septic systems average between $10k and $12k for a two or three bed home. That is what we went for in the design. We hired a septic engineer to take the surveys we had, overlay the approximate locations of the build sites and lay out the systems. They came out to do what's called a soil percolation (perc) test to test the quality of the soil and determine it would support the systems we wanted to install for each house.

Each of the ten lots passed the perc test, we had confirmation from the city that we could extend the water main, and we submitted our subdivision plan to the State of Arkansas.

Then it was rejected. Not one time. Not five times. *Nine times.*

Here is where the importance of proper planning comes into play. In hindsight, we should have hired a civil engineering firm to work up the entire plan for us from surveys, to water layout and septic design. It would have cost more up front but it would have saved us a ton of time and stress. Instead, we planned based on what we were told by the local water department and the company we hired to do the septic plan. The septic engineer told us early in the initial planning stages that he was qualified to design and submit subdivision plans to the state. The installer at the water department told us we could avoid expensive engineering fees if we hired him directly to design and install the new water main.

We connected the water department to the septic engineer and they submitted the plan. After waiting three weeks for the state to review the first application, it was denied with a note indicating that they needed further clarification. The water department coordinated with the septic engineer to make the changes they felt the state needed to see and the plan was resubmitted to the state. Three more weeks went by waiting on the health department to review and it was once again sent back to us a notice requesting further clarification.

This process repeated itself for months with little to no progress. We had written confirmation from the local health department that the project has been approved. We had a letter from the water department indicating that they would provide municipal water service for the development. The state health department verbally indicated that the plan looked good but they continued to drag out the final approval pending the written revisions they were requesting.

Each time we would make the revisions requested by the state, they would request new revisions to some other component of the plan.

We came to find out that the service who was handling our subdivision application had never done one involving a municipal water main expansion before. The contact we were working with from the water department was submitting drawings of their proposed water main in a different format from the septic engineer. Additionally, the survey we had conducted to show the easements for the new water line didn't line up to the original plan proposed within the septic layout. The representative from the state would process our application to the point where he would encounter an item that needed to be clarified but would then stop and return the application to us. Each time the application was returned, it was an average three week turn around time before they would review it again.

Had we consulted with an engineering firm that specialized in this type of development, they would have likely foreseen the issues that kept our application from being approved for so long.

We would have had a better understanding of the hard costs associated with building out the project and we would have shaved several months off of the process.

We learned a lot on this project. Ultimately, it worked out quite well.

We purchased the property for $286,000 in June of 2023.

By September of 2024 we had all ten lots sold for a total of $599,000 (average $59,900 per acre).

We sold another eight acre tract in October of 2024 for $225,000.

Total sales of $824,000.

We spent approximately $50,000 on surveys, initial clearing, engineering and other miscellaneous expenses associated with marketing and sales. We then set aside $65,000 to cover the water main expansion.

Our final net after accounting for the initial investment and expenses came out to $423,000. Not a bad return for a little over a year.

About Ryan Duffy

Ryan Duffy is a real estate developer specializing in unique short term rental properties near Branson, Missouri. Licensed in Missouri, Arkansas, and Oklahoma, his brokerage Duffy Homes Realty assists clients in the sales and acquisitions of investment properties. His property management group, Ozark Mountain Vacation, provides five star hospitality utilizing a balance of technology and in-person attention. As a licensed home builder, his company Duffy Homes LLC provides customized development plans to create one of a kind builds and innovative subdivision planning. Ryan lives in North Arkansas with his amazing wife\business partner Shae and their three children (Gavin, Lana, and Jack).

Find out more about Duffy Homes by visiting: https://linktr.ee/duffyhomes

MAKE YOUR W2 OPTIONAL, NOT REQUIRED

by Andrew Boer

L ife was good. I was a husband and father. We owned our own home that we ourselves remodeled. I drove what I wanted. My wife, Toni, drove what she wanted. We went on vacations when we wanted. We were proficient at discussing the difference between wants and needs for our children. What else could we ask for out of life? The short answer is A LOT.

I earned a living in Civil Engineering, educating engineers and municipalities about what innovative polymers existed to make our nation's underground infrastructure more robust and foolproof. I identified early on that a sales position paid more than any engineering design role. I worked my way up from Inside Sales to Global Sales Manager over a 12-year career. That's when it hit me. The top isn't what it's all cracked up to be.

We earned a comfortable living, but I didn't want to work solely for the financial benefit of my employer. Creative strategies on my end turned into millions on theirs, but that was what was expected of me. The pay was not commensurate with the output. That's when I knew something had to change. The VERY NEXT bonus, we WERE going to change things.

In December 2020, we bought a 4 bed/1.5 bath Farmhouse on the Kentucky Bourbon Trail. The next few months were cold and stressful, as we turned it into a 3 Bed/2.5 bath Farmhouse to put on AirBnB. AirDNA forecasted it making $34k per year. That was enough to cover the mortgage, so we were going to look at it like Long Term Rental Investors as we enjoyed the house being paid for by others and going up in value over time.

In April 2021, we listed it on a Tuesday and the first guest showed up on Friday. We got paid on Monday. We quickly learned that the majority of guests booked their stay during "pillow talk" at night as our cell phone notifications went off as we were falling asleep, but it was the sound of success. Money was literally pouring in over text messages.

We are glad to report that our houses outperform those same projections by 100% on average as our $34k forecast ended with $68k its first year. That led to an extra $3k per month profit to our already comfortable living. That is AFTER we increased the value of the home from $205k to $350k in 4 months. That led to us recouping ALL of our initial investment (down payment, renovation, and furnishing costs). That's when we knew we were on to something. Today, we're able to buy homes WITHOUT a paycheck, remodel quickly, furnish quickly, and earn MUCH MORE than $3k per month.

Short Term Rentals became our focus because I enjoyed the forced appreciation through renovations, while my wife THRIVED with her acumen for interior design and hospitality. I appeared as a real estate flipper by getting homes renovated into 5 star "scroll stoppers." That's because we're working to get a potential guest to stop scrolling on AirBnB and view our listings in more detail in a market where there could be hundreds of competitors WITH ONE SINGLE HERO PHOTO.

My personal passion is converting excess square footage, where it makes sense, into additional bedrooms or bathrooms. We want to allow larger groups to stay at our properties, but understand that it's not just one family. We believe that no more than 4 people should share a bathroom and that their bathroom shouldn't require a flight of stairs. That has led to losing a bedroom in a 4 bed / 1.5 bath to turn into a 3 bed / 2.5 bath for guest comfort.

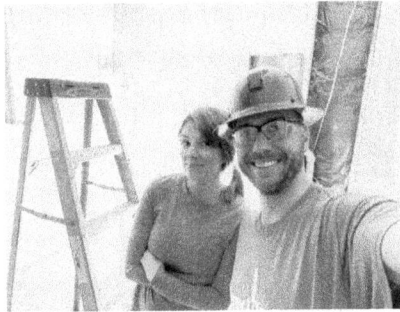

*Husband/Wife Together Turning
Her Passion into Their Realty*

We have also converted 240 square feet of crawlspace into a stunning basement bathroom for two bedrooms that would have required a flight of stairs. It took a week of digging by hand, footings, cinder blocks, and waterproofing before we even got to start the plumbing. No one will ever know it used to be a cold, wet crawl space unless they look in the utility closet where we put a tankless water heater, sump pump, and crawlspace access.

We are STR investors because we enjoy three investment benefits: Forced Appreciation, Appreciation, and Positive Monthly Cash Flow.

Forced Appreciation is increasing the value of the home significantly in a short amount of time by significant remodeling. Appreciation is the home increasing in value over time due to the sheer limited nature of land. Positive Monthly Cash Flow is the cherry on top as the home earns more than it costs to operate. That delta between the two can be THOUSANDS of dollars per month. This last investment benefit can be what makes your W2 Career, W2 Optional.

One investment that made strides for us started in December 2021. We purchased an abandoned house filled with someone's belongings who had passed away, NOT IN THE HOUSE. We put 15% down on $89,900 and four months, plus $40k in renovations, later had a house worth $260k. That $130k investment produced a $130k profit. It also produced $69k per year for two years as a Premier Short Term Rental in the area.

In October 2023, it became apparent to my wife and I that it was fiscally irresponsible for me to stay employed as a W2 employee. I was salaried, which created a layer of guilt whenever I wasn't contemplating civil engineering, even though no one is expected to work 100 hours a week. The psychological strain of serving two roles was too much. Toni and I put our heads together and agreed that although the pay was strong by society's standards; it came at an opportunity cost that couldn't be ignored.

It is a treat to share our success with others on a myriad of social media platforms. LinkedIn drove my career with success for over a decade. Recruiters made an impact on the livelihood of our household and your work is often unappreciated, but please know, You Are Appreciated. However, today I use LinkedIn as a portal to journal our investment strategies and it has created a multitude of AMAZING relationships that began due to our industry, but has crafted friendships that would flourish on a level that civil engineering would not provide.

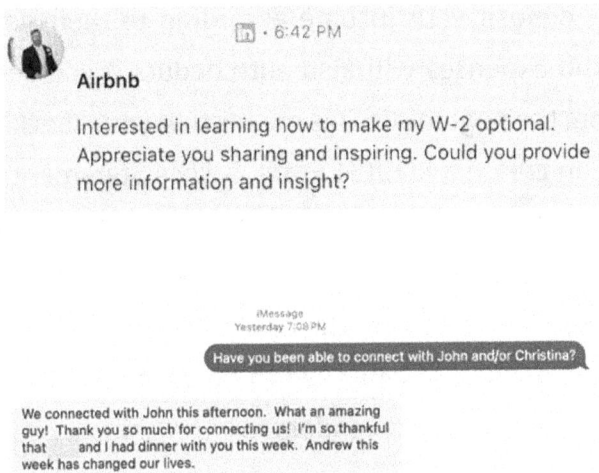

Airbnb · 6:42 PM

Interested in learning how to make my W-2 optional. Appreciate you sharing and inspiring. Could you provide more information and insight?

iMessage
Yesterday 7:08 PM

Have you been able to connect with John and/or Christina?

We connected with John this afternoon. What an amazing guy! Thank you so much for connecting us! I'm so thankful that   and I had dinner with you this week. Andrew this week has changed our lives.

My Top 5 Lessons If I Had to Start All Over Again

David Letterman's Top 10 was A HIT in my house growing up, but for the sake of brevity for this book, I'd like to share my Top 5 Recommendations for anyone beginning their STR venture.

5. Start a separate checking account for each property you own

Accounting and Bookkeeping is CRITICAL for your success. Getting things set up right from the start will make your life SO MUCH EASIER. I will let others address who owns the house and checking account, which refers to whether it is you on a personal level or if a business is being created/used to purchase the house. That is a legal discussion, which is better served by someone other than me.

The internet has made this so much easier than "our ancestors" had it. Short Term Rental Platforms such as AirBnB and VRBO will directly deposit your income according to their policies. Your mortgage and expenses will also auto deduct if you set things up correctly from the beginning. This means that your checking account statement can create a ROUGH Profit & Loss Statement if your self discipline will force you to use the correct debit card for the correct application. That means you need to have that checking account setup BEFORE closing to wire the cash to close on closing day. Your house specific debit card will need to be used for Amazon, Wayfair, Overstock and all the other vendors for furnishings.

4. Walk through a property before you buy it as if you are the guest

If you can envision staying in the property as a guest, you're going to be much better off. It's midnight and you need to use the restroom. Where are the lights? How far do you have to walk?

You just got out of the hot tub, where will you change from your wet swimsuit into dry clothes? Do you have to walk across tile that's going to become incredibly slippery?

You just got back from a day of Bourbon Distillery Tours. You have a headache because the Bourbon Tastings are INCREDIBLY generous and they start pouring like that before 9am. Where will you want to kick back and relax before dinner becomes the next big topic?

Focus on what you would prefer and then ask yourself if that is specific to you, or do your friends agree? Consensus helps virtually everyone make decisions confidently. Ask around. This small act also tells your friends that you're open to suggestions. YOU WANT SUGGESTIONS! If you're not changing, you're stagnant and your listing will always need improvement as well.

3. Add Value that no one else saw

These could be things such as a second living room becoming a bedroom, a crawlspace becoming a bathroom, or losing a bedroom for another bathroom if there's more than four adults being asked to share 1 toilet, shower, and vanity.

These are going to surface when you envision yourself staying there. Do you want to use the same restroom as 7 other people? Probably not. Increasing the number of bedrooms and bathrooms is a surefire way to increase the value of your house.

If you have 4 bedrooms, but only 1 bathroom. You might want to sacrifice a bedroom for a second bathroom. It seems counterintuitive to most, but I want our guests to enjoy themselves for positive monthly cash flow more than I focus on an appraisal that only comes up when I'm refinancing or selling.

2. Plan Your Work and Work Your Plan

I've loved this phrase for over a decade and relying on it gives me confidence that we minimize our risk by putting our ideas on paper. What's the difference between a thought and a plan? Pen and paper. A plan doesn't exist until something gets written down.

Microsoft Excel allows me to numerically calculate down payment, mortgage payment, monthly cash flow, cash out, equity, and so much more. Fields being auto-populated with formulas makes our lives as investors so simple.

1. Only work with a Real Estate Agent who is a Short Term Rental Investor As Well

It's been said that over 80% of Licensed Real Estate Agents nationally didn't earn a dollar last year. That tells you how many people go through the training, but don't have the experience. Short Term Rentals are NOTHING like families moving homes. Our purchases SHOULD NOT be emotional. We are usually not concerned about the local schools, colleges being a notable exception. Our business requires CAREFUL CONSIDERATION of Local Short Term Rental Regulations.

Markets are different from county to county, or even neighborhood to neighborhood. Homeowners Associations have more ability to regulate than the county, so we avoid homes governed by one. Local regulations are often created to restrict the desire for Short Term Rental Investors such as 6 day or 30 day minimum night stays. Counties can create the need for a Conditional Use Permit, which even if all boxes are checked, a subjective Board of Adjustment

Board can deny you leaving you high and dry with an expensive house and no use.

Your Short Term Rental University never stops and having someone who walks your walk and talks your talk is invaluable. YouTube is a fantastic tool, but as a construction savvy individual; I would argue 75% of the content on there is bad information. It worked for them, but someone that worked for me once called my ingenuity out once and said "Could you? Sure. The question is Should You?" Thanks John.

It is not a fictitious idea that your first investment property will change your finances forever. This is a fact if you plan your work and work your plan. The unknown is scary, but it doesn't have to be. W2 Optional is a thought that I'm seeking to turn into a movement. There are so many living paycheck to paycheck, which robs us of the freedom to make critical life decisions because of BILLS. I want to empower you to work there BECAUSE YOU WANT TO, not because YOU HAVE TO.

LinkedIn is my primary social media platform and I can assure you that a DM there will be read by me. It also gives you a glimpse into my thoughts by reviewing past posts. Most DMs will lead to a face to face Zoom for us to learn more about each other. I want you to know that I'm taking the call because my family's financial future is changed for generations to come and yours can too. It does take work, but you can do it and I'm willing to do the work with you. I'm also straight forward, so those that know me best know that I voice opinions that your friends probably wouldn't share.

Accountability drove me to new heights a decade ago and I'm

here to break down mental barriers with you. I invite you AND your spouse on that intro call. The likelihood of success without both of you on board is virtually zero. My wife pitched the Short Term Rental idea to me in 2020. I had the renovation experience and we fell into the best environment possible because she voiced her passion and we both made it work.

I'd like to say Thank You to my wife for pushing us in a direction that I never would have ventured down without her. She is the secret weapon to our success. This formula started small and has made its way to something that REQUIRES a lot of people on a daily and weekly basis. As a husband, I want to provide for my wife, but for what she covers, it takes others. Thank you to Jen, Jeff, Michelle, Cassidy, Melissa, and more for having my wife's back. Thank you to Gus, Nelson, Josh, Kyle, Dale, Marcus, James, Brian, Damien, and more for having our back to renovate these homes into "Scrollstoppers."

It takes time for your "Tribe" to be developed. A few of those names aren't with us anymore for one reason or another. However, we all have seasons of life and being open to meeting new people has forever changed ours.

About Andrew Boer

ANDREW L. BOER is a construction aficionado and founder of Built of Bourbon, the premier remodeler on The Kentucky Bourbon Trail.

His short term rental investments started as his W2 bonuses went into real estate while many of his colleagues bought boats. Three years later, he retired from the civil engineering industry before the age of 40 to keep up with the demand for luxury short term rentals in Central Kentucky. He and his wife, Toni, have dedicated their careers to empowering others to reap the same financial rewards.

His civil engineering background serves his clients well. Built for Bourbon converts more land and unfinished square footage into finished space than any other residential contractor in the region.

Bathroom additions, remodels, garage conversions, and outbuilding renovations are at the forefront of his services. He maintains high standards, using his personal investments as an inspiration. His clients are given the same level of luxury and care he gives his own assets.

BfB completes a project and launches a Short Term Rental every 2 weeks on average, with as many as ten projects open every week. Andrew is a faith based CEO, husband to Toni, and father of five.

https://linktr.ee/andrewlboer

DEFINITIONS

by Cash Street Advisors Press

Real Estate Education: Building a Foundation of Knowledge

In the ever-evolving world of real estate, knowledge is power. This chapter is designed to equip you with a comprehensive understanding of key terms and concepts essential for success in the industry. Whether you're a novice or a seasoned investor, mastering these definitions will serve as a solid foundation for navigating the complexities of real estate investing.

Adjustable-Rate Mortgage (ARM): A mortgage loan with an interest rate that may change periodically based on changes in a specified index.

Appreciation: The increase in the value of a property over time.

Buyer's Market: A market condition in which there are more properties for sale than there are buyers, giving buyers the upper hand in negotiations.

Cap Rate (Capitalization Rate): The rate of return on areal estate investment property based on the income that the property is expected to generate.

Cash Flow: The net income generated by a real estate investment after expenses have been deducted.

Closing Costs: The fees and expenses associated with finalizing a real estate transaction, paid by both the buyer and seller.

Debt Service: The amount of money required to cover the repayment of principal and interest on a loan.

Down Payment: The initial payment made by a buyer towards the purchase price of a property.

Equity: The difference between the market value of a property and the amount of debt owed on it.

Escrow: A neutral third party that holds funds and documents on behalf of the buyer and seller until the completion of a real estate transaction.

Fair Market Value: The price at which a property would sell under normal market conditions, determined by factors such as location, condition, and demand.

Foreclosure: The legal process by which a lender repossesses a property from a borrower who has defaulted on their mortgage payments.

Gentrification: The process of revitalizing and improving a neighborhood, often resulting in the displacement of lower-income residents.

Gross Income: The total income generated by a property before expenses are deducted.

Homeowners Association (HOA): An organization responsible for managing and maintaining common areas and amenities in a residential community, funded by homeowner dues.

HUD(Housing and Urban Development): A government agency responsible for implementing federal housing policies and programs.

Inflation: The rate at which the general level of prices for goods and services is rising, eroding purchasing power over time.

Interest Rate: The rate at which interest is charged on a loan.

Joint Venture: A business arrangement in which two or more parties agree to pool their resources and expertise to undertake a specific project or investment.

Lease: A contractual agreement between a landlord and a tenant, granting the tenant the right to occupy a property for a specified period in exchange for rent.

Lien: A legal claim against a property as security for the repayment of a debt.

Market Analysis: An assessment of the current and potential future market conditions for a particular property or location.

Multiple Listing Service (MLS): A database used by real estate professionals to list and search for properties available for sale or rent.

Net Operating Income (NOI): The total income generated by a property after operating expenses have been deducted.

Option: A contractual agreement giving one party the right, but not the obligation, to buy or sell a property at a specified price within a specified period.

PITI(Principal, Interest, Taxes, Insurance): The components of a mortgage payment, including principal, interest, property taxes, and homeowner's insurance.

Principal: The original amount of money borrowed in a loan, excluding interest.

Quitclaim Deed: A legal document transferring the ownership of a property from one party to another, without guaranteeing the title's validity.

Real Estate Investment Trust (REIT): A company that owns, operates, or finances income-generating real estate, often traded on major stock exchanges.

Rehabilitation: The process of renovating or restoring a property to improve its condition and value.

Short Sale: A real estate transaction in which the proceeds from selling a property fall short of the balance owed on the mortgage, requiring lender approval to accept less than the full amount owed.

Subprime Mortgage: A mortgage loan offered to borrowers with poor credit histories, typically carrying higher interest rates and fees.

Tax Lien: A claim imposed by the government against a property owner who has failed to pay property taxes.

Title Insurance: Insurance that protects the buyer or lender against defects in the title of a property.

Underwriting: The process by which a lender evaluates the credit-worthiness of a borrower and determines whether to approve a loan.

Upzoning: The process of rezoning land to allow for higher-density development, increasing its potential value.

Vacancy Rate: The percentage of rental units that are unoccupied in a particular area at a given time.

Vacant Land: Land that is not currently being used or developed.

Walkthrough: A final inspection of a property conducted by the buyer before closing to ensure that it is in the agreed-upon condition.

Zoning: Government regulations that dictate how land can be used and developed within a specific area.

CONCLUSION

by Cash Street Advisors Press

A s we reach the end of this journey together, we want to express my deepest gratitude for joining us on this exploration of the thrilling world of real estate. Whether you're just beginning your journey or you've been on this path for some time, we hope you've found inspiration, guidance, and practical insights to propel you forward.

Remember, success in real estate is not just about financial gain—it's about creating opportunities, building relationships, and leaving a lasting impact on the world around us. As you embark on your own real estate adventure, we encourage you to embrace the lessons learned, seize the opportunities that come your way, and always strive to make a positive difference in the lives of others.

Your journey in real estate is just beginning, and the possibilities are endless. So go forth with confidence, determination, and a relentless pursuit of excellence.

Your future in real estate awaits—make it extraordinary.

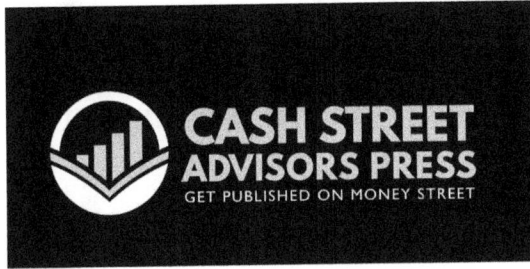

About Cash Street Advisors Press

Cash Street Advisors Press is committed to empowering authors like you to embark on an extraordinary publishing journey through sharing stories of financial and time freedom. Our mission is to bring these stories to life and provide them with the platform they deserve. What sets us apart is our commitment to being more than just a publishing house. We're your partners, your cheerleaders, and your guides as you navigate the path to becoming a published author. Our team is dedicated to nurturing your literary ambitions and helping you shape a brighter future through your words.

Don't wait for the right moment—create it. Your story deserves to be told, and we're here to help you tell it in the most impactful way possible. *Are you ready to get published on Money Street?*

Visit us at:
https://cashstreetpublishing.com/

CREATING A LIFE OF ABUNDANCE

Ready to be in Business with your spouse?

Unlock the secrets to abundance with *Creating a Life of Abundance* – a multi-award-winning Amazon best-selling book that has captivated readers worldwide! Join the inspiring journeys of four extraordinary couples as they navigate the path to prosperity and fulfillment.

Proven Strategies: Discover actionable steps to manifest abundance in every aspect of your life.

Couples in Business: Are you intrigued by the idea of working with your spouse? Dive into real stories and insights shared by couples who've turned their partnerships into successful ventures.

Elevate Your Life: Whether you're seeking financial freedom, stronger relationships, or a thriving business with your spouse – this book is your guide to creating a life filled with abundance.

Act Now! Your path to abundance starts here. Embark on a transformative journey with "Creating a Life of **ABUNDANCE**."

Buy Now! Available on Amazon!
https://cashstreettech.com/store/

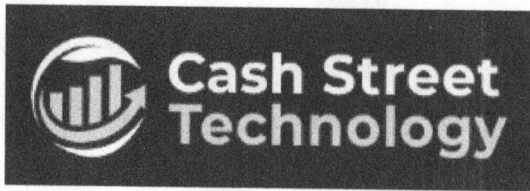

CASH STREET TECHNOLOGY

How Can We Serve You?

At Cash Street Technology, our purpose is to collaborate with small business owners, property managers, real estate investors and entrepreneurs. We are laser focused on financial literacy and providing business owners, couples and individuals educational materials needed to succeed. Each year we host various retreats, coaching and offer monthly masterminds.

MEN'S MASTERMIND

Expand your network, share knowledge, and collaborate for collective success. Each member is a valuable asset, contributing unique expertise and support.

COUPLES WEALTH & HEALTH RETREAT

Exclusive experience tailored for couples navigating the challenges of busy and demanding lives. Leave refreshed, armed with actionable plans for your family's financial future.

ONE-ON-ONE COACHING

Tailored strategies, individual attention, and goal-focused support for your unique journey.

https://cashstreettech.com/

Duffy Homes

Duffy Homes Realty is the go-to brokerage for investing in the Ozarks. Their small group of highly trained agents are uniquely qualified to assist you in reaching your investment goals. Licensed in Arkansas, Missouri and Oklahoma, they specialize in luxury lake-front, short term rentals and commercial properties. Their agents have first hand experience in new construction, short term rental management, remodeling, interior design and land development.

Visit Duffy Homes at:
https://linktr.ee/duffyhomes